Rafetown Georgics

Rafetown Georgics

Garin Cycholl

For Celia —
Finally getting this to you,
in appreciation of your
visit and the
entrancing songs of
Cherokee Bend Kill!
Hoping our paths
cross again soon!
Best,
Garin

Cracked
Slab

BOOKS

Chicago 2008

ISBN 0-9786440-2-6

First Edition

cover photo: Tabitha Ostermann

Cracked Slab Books
PO BOX 1070
Oak Park, IL 60302

http://www.crackedslabbooks.com

Table of Contents

The Drama of Objects

"Epic Problems and Their Solutions"	11
Pantoum	12
"The Americans"	13
"Travels through North and South Carolina"	21
sand fort	23
"Museum for a Small City"	25
Long Songs of North Carolina	27
"Fld.wrk"	29

Bird at Camarillo

Blues—Silences—Stops Between	37
"Crazy Woman with Two Cats"	41
why not then—buy	43
36 on 6 by Michael Anania	44
"Town Hall Concert"	46
Much New Jazz	48
"Eleanor"	50
"Chicago 53"	51

Rafetown Georgics

Antebellum Christi	57
"Midwestern Landscape #13"	58
"Midwestern Landscape #110"	60
"Midwestern Landscape #190"	61
Dundas and Rafetown, 1997	62
Farmers and Merchants Bank	64
"Midwestern Landscape #11"	66
"Midwestern Landscape #172"	67
"Midwestern Landscape #2"	68
"Midwestern Landscape #9"	69
The Book of Frogs	70

Levitations, the Pleasures and Terrors of

Topics in Experimental Photography	75
"Snapshot of Wallace Stevens in His Garden"	77

Levitations   80
"Hymn to Aphrodite"   82
Three for Rita Figueroa   84
Country & Western   86
not leafy or jazzsprung   88
Seven-Headed Luther   90
flames   flames flames   92

About the Author   97

Acknowledgments   97

Index of Titles   98

The Drama of Objects

"Epic Problems and Their Solutions"

Look here, he'd fuck up a one-car funeral.

If you are out alone in the starry night, wandering
among the troops, then what brings you? If the Interior
Secretary enters, then the paper drops to the floor. If dancing
is censored, is it my fault? The statistical heart. If phallo-
centrism, then the king. If Homer comes to the lunch, open
another jar of orange marmalade. If the rhetoricians' hall
of fame calls, tell them Yeltsin is busy. If the eye is the
problem, then why not the ear, thumb, or kneecap? Cold
corpus collosum. Who came to the window? If
phallocentrism, then the queen. Oh, the goddamned
dishes. If familiarity breeds contempt, then it's goodbye,
pork pie hat. If children's voices bounce off snowflakes or
Albion brick. If Kristy Odelius comes to call, the oranges are
in danger. If biscuits, then beans. If Brook Bute, then
the box of frogs. If the string breaks, then gray speckled bird
is out of the question. Trial by seashore. If the clock is
beyond the light, then leaded panes and de Chirico. If it
proposes without inventing, please consult "Thought, *a
discussion of.*" If we are talking *fruit* now.

Pantoum

Ah, sunshine!
Eyes do little here;
we'll huddle together.
More or less continually at war,

eyes do little. Here,
salt winds locked
more or less continually. At war,
we sing hymns to the yellow gods,

salt winds. Locked
in the estuaries' passing,
we sing hymns to the yellow. Gods
hunker in the tides left between time

in the estuaries, passing
into cordgrass. Our eyes swim and
hunker in the tides left. Between time
and not, rest here.

Into cordgrass, our eyes swim and
see in the marsh
and not rest. Here,
trace the skin between your fingers.

See! In the marsh,
eelgrass strands bleed salt.
Trace the skin. Between your fingers,
these grasses don't say a goddamned thing.

Eelgrass strands bleed. Salt!
Ah, sunshine!
These grasses! Don't say a goddamned thing.
We'll huddle together.

The Americans

after Robert Frank

(Motorama—Los Angeles)

it's never jazz
playing as you
cross Anaconda
to Blackfoot but
a Denver talk show
host, "That boy is
red, I tell you" green
constellations   *light*
seeps in from the
past

      yellowing

alive and awake
outside Omaha; it's
2 A.M.

(Candy store—New York City)

music oranged   she
is talking   he hears
it   now song then
colors   some great
Chrysler disembodied
and floating   like some
medieval ceremony an
ochred New York
cocktail party cigars
blueing air   *the music*
blacks and thickens

(Indianapolis)

as though waiting, men
with shirts untucked   the
woman's eyes and metals
tucked into bike's shine
feet tucked below saddle
seat and "Hop on, now"

I speak of things that
are everywhere—easily
found   the Big Distance
and all that goddamned
chrome

     (how she reads motion in the dark

(Assembly line—Detroit)

two boys at a Michigan drive-in

       —If my car were a woman, I'd fuck it.
       —She knows how to walk, that one.

then out to Belle Isle cans emptied
of Stag and Spam soldier's knees
crooked against bark paper plates
at the roots meats triangulated and
opened pinked and snacked *flags!*
lilied or frayed pillowed canopied or
hung backwards *the stainless steel*
and the woman are real, but her
mouth is not

(Mississippi River, Baton Rouge, Louisiana)

(how light works along water

against crosses, grasses, water and
asphalt things tabbed plastic blooms
jukebox eye among small sticks left by
mourners the Jesus hooked mercilessly
to its terrain

(U.S. 91, leaving Blackfoot, Idaho)

The most dangerous thing to do is to stand still.

A man in a black t-shirt drives a green pick-up.

The radio quit somewhere north of Rexburg.

Yesterday was a day of mirrors.

He's been driving all night.

Even in the headlights, the colors fail.

(View from a hotel window—Butte, Montana)

(how it is to awaken to running

hey ding ding
hey diddle
ding ding
and

bombs

and

bombs

and

bombs

no pleasures
or terrors but
levitation the
Big Distance
and all this god-
damned chrome
that's the myth
in America—that
things move

Mercury
Impala
Corvair

Nomad
Eldorado
Rambler

there are little

places to break
down all over
this land

Travels through North and South Carolina

It generally ends in voluntary banishment. And it's these
renegades and vagabonds who commit depredations and murders
on the frontier.

Life is an astonishing thing,

                              she
said   certain mischievous women and
chocolate   dried radish leaves smoking
monkeys hot-cooked greens and my erotic
nine iron   O, sore-lipped historians,
you sing the breath of me   I only use
my breath for laughter now   Let my
spirit go   I want to see the comedians of
my youth grainy black-and-white voices
and stock laughter   the product of some trance-
like state   film fluttering on the page

                                        We
will not; we cannot. We want you here.

but I'm no thinking frog   Tennessee's got new
mythological machinery   talking to me talking
to me talking

                    like a wildflower
                    like certain secret ministries
                    like nymphaea nelumbo

they are talking to me too   every week the same
goddamned thing   preacher says,

                         the sea
giving up its dead; the fountains of the deep again

breaking up

        all that's left of me ambition   snow
pushed to the corner under the walls on a bed of clay
and gravel

sand fort

a shadow georgic

after her gorilla coat had been stolen,
how Richard's mother had ordered the
line of palms planted in her Stamford
foyer—trunks deadened by the trip up
from Jupiter, they began their slow rot
under Albany glass and curiously bent
black metal—the landscaper speaking
from her widow's walk—"Ma'am, we
can't do it in March—it'll kill 'em."

sand fort
                    or "sent forth," grains
pour from his opened mouth—
pilgrims sing of it, haul
their songs home from heaven,
voices clean as polished steel—
or burned in the ground—*one
who is buried and speaks thick-
ly is lost*

                    in that world, it's always
blacked blood speaking from the
sand
            (why we must sink *a
labyrinth broken open from above
or worn away at its foundations*

survey the quantities and types of
sand disposed—deregulate foundry
waste sands or figure the monied
implications of reuse   "offered a
commission, you must choose
between the living and the dead"

although the poem itself tells us that
vipers are found in a variety of shapes
and sizes what grows in sand?   cells
hungry beyond all need the winds
pile up and lakes empty themselves;
the subsurface creep bought and
sold as a matter of routine genius—

imagine your old man come home
as a pig
                or "night falling
like honey" but what death is
cooked in the thicket? the city
tumbling down, an old drunk
pissing in the dust

"Museum for a Small City"

the 15th of 1000 manifestoes

We wanted to raise a new Omaha, carrying
our memory around in blocks of wood, red
shades, and outposts, listening. He picked
up a trumpet. "Thank you, Mr. Eastman!"
you said. "I am painting with light." That's
all—a place where we could play with light,
dissemble it, note the shades overhead. "If
the modern is taking apart—" he said, but
the horn interrupted him. Sun murky, then
sharp. "I'm as much a part of the world as
that missing plank on the train platform," he
said, slick with how bars move across sound.

cooked roots
cadaverous waters
some great city
poet with his radio
uncovered leaving
town with all I
could carry the
same old men
waiting *bright*
boy, bright boy
or if the myth
gets pushed into
itself, what'll
come up out
of the soil the
water the light
falling men
sown in the
grass beside
the highway

dark knots in
the grass slender
dubloons sunk in
train rides out
west chums and
hombres, embracing
statues, four-beat
licks, nostalgia for
the box and
writing on the
backs of photo-
graphs then words
over scallops, over
drowned horses
bird nesting in
dust pollination
by the wind

"This is the last museum," you said. "Who
designed it, but me?" Yet small engines are
working, recalcitrant particles, credit sickness;
how the numbers don't add up. First, there's a
hallway, then a window, then a set of stairs. The
woman then, carrying her memory in horns, sun-
light, and a black-and-chrome Toronado. We'd
have sent a ride, if you'd asked it.

Long Songs of North Carolina

i.   Breakwater and shadows,
      delicate and submerged.
      Angers swim in a carbon sea.

ii.   Strandlines and gulls poking
      holes in the grit. Salt-pruned
      sea oats, smeared by wind.

iii.   Surface creep and sea rocket,
      slacks, common frog fruit.
      A mile of spray in my eye.

iv.   Backdunes and panic grass.
      Floppy sand in two o'clock light,
      crossing my tracks with dogprints.

v.   Highway 12. Driving the Chevy
down to Duck. *Oh, blue-eyed fish-
monger, what d'you have for me today?*

vi.   Dredge zone and spoil. Tangling
railroad vine and fishbones. Broom-
sedge reaching its northern limit.

vii.   Sea foam pulled back, sound
and stilt songs grassing.
Feed me to their myths.

Fld.wrk

for Irene Siegel

moon west by Virginia creeper—
all this digging gets to me—"you
can't go around threatening the
old gods," he said—the seeds go
half a fingertip into the soil, fed
with care, gently tilled

I'm weighing Nick Andreas'
brain in my open palm—it thinks,
"Persia"—it thinks, "code in the
beans"—it thinks, "open road" a
practical wisdom—don't drip
melon juice into the soil—or
some other counterfeit land-
scape; planting by almanac

DeKalb

        Asgrow

                Agrigold

2

his lying memo—*the
soil's metallic taste. . .*

the hedge is a lie is
an invention of the high
command is an illness
among the troops

planted in gray soil, the
crows are descending—
the line between us, an
industrial corridor

but we were giving the
city back to the prairie—
estates, my true calling

> *how to scrub the soil*
> *how to wash the slake*
> *how to cut the checks*

among the fencerows,
the man's voice crying,
"cut the bacteria out of
my foot; cut the moon-
light out of my eye"

3

taking apart the shed with ropes and a
maul   mint green diamonds on cheap white
barn paint   "by the time we'd arrived, the
house was already in an advanced state of
decay"   things changing states   the walls
and soil liquefying roots boiling with nails

kids were jumping freshly dug graves in
the spring night Callison's homer lands
among palms I'd given up inspecting my
line of tomato plants, a twine singing with
emptied Pabst cans (like Virgil himself,
things strung to ward off the crows

the collectivity of us—
pruners, those who
worked in weeds, wind
and water men

bags of lime and
pepper   skins
square
with
the
dusk

4

"Persian gardens"
planted at midnight,
the daisies cut me—
among fencerows, a
glimpse of stars
between rains

5

We called it O'Leary's line—thirty
foot shoots of blue stem ringing the
city—an idea conceived as he did a
quarter-mile belly crawl through Indiana
limestone—the city now gone under-
ground—the farmer poses along some
ancient ridge—regarding the vista, he
sees the city from a distance—the soil
owns him

                    owns the air

                              owns the

          lake, green

                    glass smashed

                              along its shoreline

          6

          put your hand to plow at its
          tip, yellows congealing we
          are like red frogs drawn to
          the camera

          I'd always imagined myself
          as necessary like some
          emergency blacksmith
          service   a clip-
          board and tools but
          as of Friday, I've
          become colored
          glass dimpled and
          spilled among
          Bibb seed

          in the middle of
          it all okra the
          greener
          line   fixed
          bayonets

                    cameo

7

hell, the

      whole   prairie's

tired

8

cutting trenches after
a heavy rain we
found a love letter:
I'm not your fucking
doorman, the one who
pulls back boughs
for your flat socket-
less eyes

9

or I could be a major's tongue, a
sharpening stone—then there's
the smell of smoke—prescribed
burns before December—how
he evaporates in the ash

10

opening the floodgates of greenery)
you can burn money he asked, "do
you think it burns green? it don't, it
burns blue—the sulfites in the inks in
the green in the paper—the shit's
                        (currency
poisonous—
you ever
tried to
eat a
sawbuck?"

Bird at Camarillo

Blues—Silences—Stops Between

for Sterling Plumpp

i. "Boplicity"

Guys play it off, circle the square. It's
the man born in

American sound that's remembered. What
happened to space—

Arkansas adding a kind of running finger
piano. Geography—bad

gospels, exploration, and no mercies. Western
woman running the sun

like a tomahawk. But you and I could get into
the sound's space—something

that sounded like the feeling I had when the land
was running out the blood.

It was hell, large and becoming a people, their
triumphs are muscled jet. Ahab

was no beginning, no barrier to the command of
one story. You wrote

five bars of road—a stretch of earth, half sea, half
land—a high ride on such space.

ii. "On Green Dolphin Street"

like a piano heard over the pay-
phone from Sutherland's *that
kind of stretched out sound* all
those ears looking for space

*how many times it escaped thru
a crack in the wall*—the piano
had it right—trading riffs of the
sound relenting, leaving mythy

spaces *why every blues is a
walking blues* your sound's edge
against it, stillness staking its
places across broken measures

how did you hear them? trading
silences with Miles *riffing and
riffing your name* thru Mississippi,
Chicago, the stops between

iii. "Blue in Green"

the sound that's plucked or the sound that's blown
the myth in the fingertips, the blues in the howl
the sharp lip of a bloom, the horn's rolled bell
how sound fills a terrain or a room on S. Indiana
the old man on drums, the young one on trumpet
the blue in the green or the green in the blue some-
thing about walking on hardened feet, long song

iv. "Bitches Brew"

This is a con-
certo, right? a
fugue or a mo-
tif we bounced

footnotes or chop
suey blues a coil
revelry get up get
up get up the horn's

a memory organ
improvising what
it can't recall tre-
ading the next solo

no Mississippi dol-
drums but smoke
's shadow on a
canvass wall

"Crazy Woman with Two Cats"

They're bruising the sky again
these painters   it's not natural
          she says   *Supernatural?*

No
          stones   the bay   even palms contused
stung cheek   bled shadow
                              flat brush drug through
purple dirt   she speaks to a rash   old skins

(broken glass sound)

———

          Myself, I've had five appearances of the Virgin. One,
in the mustache of that Kentucky state trooper, wrote me up
for speeding on U.S. 60, outside Paducah. In Nahum's book,
his bag of greens. Wm Faulkner cut black paper books for his
niece. (Despite all that bourbon.) Your note. More regular in
Elsie's conch pan bread.
          Leavened. Always leavened.

———

The nature of the lesions   (bizarre shapes)
may immediately suggest artificial etiology,
but it is important to rule out every possible cause and
perform a biopsy before assigning the diagnosis of
dermatosis artefacta. The condition demands
the utmost tact on the part of the physician,
who can avert a serious outcome   (i.e. suicide)
by attempting to gain enough empathy
with the patient to ascertain the cause.

———

Picasso. He owed me money.

———

". . .(A)nd I knew that if we were going to rescue the
canvases, it was going to have to be my ass, dangling from a
rope thrown over the seacliff, sent down to get them. 'Don't
worry. I'll hold on,' Karl said. The prison doc nodded,
blessed me. 'Go with God.' So, down I started after these
landscapes that somebody'd just flung into the ocean.
'Nothing left probably!' I hollered, sounding as serious as I
could, although the rocks weren't listening. Above, Karl's
voice, 'Have you really been screwing my wife?' . . ."

———

(broken glass sound)

film winding my ankles
your hands smeared film

my feet
stretching out
world   your
skin

(untitled)

why not then—buy
a big fucking white
Lincoln and drive it to
Babylon—trade my
oily heart for technical
valor—or cruise old
North Carolina—ride
shotgun to some scrap
metal Vishnu—what
fucking question?

36 on 6 by Michael Anania

"The eye in its lifelong fidget, exact;
you wanted to say it was beginning to bother you.
Facts do not fade but are momentarily obscured,
as indistinct as water is in water.
Who was it started laughing
but ourselves, full clamorous and vain, kicking the leaves."

Light leaves
exact
shades. Laughing,
you
stand in flat water,
feet obscured

in sky. Not as along Route 13, you obscured
in my eye by light's recalled slant as it leaves
your body curled in a rented bed, but you in the calm water
of Little Grassy Lake. The photograph is exact,
its grays washed onto white paper. Not you
standing in gooseshit along the bank, laughing

as a Canadian's beak insistently taps your ankle, but laughing
as clear shade and cold sedges swim and obscure
your boots. Light becomes you
here. It visits the slick black film and leaves
what the lens has gathered. The picture could be about
                                        fucking, inexact
in its slant of bodies, but facts are facts. You're not in rolling
                                        water

but cold, flat water,
colored by sky, laughed
into being by exact
shades. How can they be obscured?
Light leaves

flecks of you.

"There must be a tune that contains this." Does it still bother
you seven years later, this reflection, standing in water
over your boots, raincoat arms dangling, leaves
dissembling around your ankles, geese laughing?
Scattered, your feet are still obscured
by sky and sedges, light's moment exact.

But you don't disappear, laughing
into flat colors of water. Obscured,
light leaves eyes' movements; its shades still exact.

"Town Hall Concert"

for Jeffery Renard Allen

*Long before he entered the world, blades of southern grass
came up through his feet.* Or taking a high ride on such space,
the sound storm is a myth. It's always some loose strain of
Dixieland that greets you, stepping down from the train.
Pieces of horn, the notes being written as they're performed.
The place made up as you step down, striding, shoe on the
rust. You look up, the sound demanding more space, let
alone time. You tell yourself the joke, the punch line already
there. The bass warms up, then the story gets on a train. *The
city bisected again & again.*

                             *He was speaking to her, saying
something about the passage over and over again. She sat at the
window watching the evening invade the avenue. Her head was
leaned against the window curtains and in her nostrils was the odor
of dusty cretonne. She was tired. She stood among the swaying
crowd in the station. The pitiful vision laid its spell.* But what
greets *you* coming down those metal steps? *This is a poem
based on actual events.* How things grow in hardscrabble. The
cement-like soil, the page; the roots, song. The story circled
and returning. "Icing this world,"

                                 he said. Two kids
coming down the block. The Impala. The playground. The
shout. The ball bouncing. The phrases not so much repeated
as retold. *Rephrased then*, the sound stung and staying high
in the ear. What was the next note? It's beyond memory but
already there in some score, howled by the world. (Try
it again.) You stole the bass, didn't you? Not the line but the
thing itself, playing it over the tops of the reeds, the brass, the
upper lips and the et cetera's. What's palmed there, what's
sown there, what's thrummed, what's lurking—

pushing back
against the sound in the strings, the fingers, the tar lake itself.
An occasional complex, like some forty-story insula, its
histories under the cover of hours, worlds dropped in like so
many details. Measured in the time it takes to get the music
from pen to stand, the train from there to the platform. The
note holds, "martyred to motion," the one great failure on the
page. Then palm slapped to bass, the voice starts again and
"it's headlines in motion," the sound moving through the
waters, the strings, the ear, the rails. *Already, the band
is warming up.*

Much New Jazz

"Liquidate the incantate."

When I understand this city
throw a stone into glassy landscape
watch it ring

Climb into my father's attic   tic   tic
tic my father's into   climb
my father

          my father
climb into   (three   four)
    father
throw a stone

Sound on my tongue
open my lips
breadbones & vinegar air; hear it !
here, it
here   something slips between
    here

          and the delta mud

(how a waterfall sets a horizon)

                              now

take the damned horn out of your mouth

———

You remember Otto Road, the fun we had
there   ascot gray sleeves gloves shed
                              your mother's red-backed corsage
that horse—

                what was its name?—kicked me in the chest
released a
cough of morning glories
                              their teeth sunk in my sadness

───────

I left your heart in San Francisco in a coat-check girl's pocket,
and in a cribnote, Tony Bennett informed me that he was now
my sworn enemy, having loved you in every city where I had
not. Hendrix strummed *Stella by Starlight*, we counted our
toes, and I'd have been more comfortable if you hadn't taken
to waving the AK-47 over your head while you talked. But
Chekhov had always read you too closely, hadn't he? True,
the actors spoke to us from the screen. That villain
embarrassed you terribly, asking you to describe your body
in twenty-five words or less. You prodded the language,
radio pricked the night air in Rothko Chapel. The dumb echo
spread inside me. I love you. Now open the goddamned
skylights.

───────

boys trees   hammer
lost in spring mud   boots
ripe for walking   red spine
flood bottoms   sounding
your voice

"Eleanor"

after Harry and Eleanor Callahan

before he'd picked up motion
pictures, they threw the city
against itself—some Eleanor, not
abstract, but substantial—some
trace of ourselves   torso
strung or flecked with bricks
or grasses—the sky gets into
it, too

        these aren't experiments
or landscapes or a matter of
words (the light never "lands"
or "uncovers" or "washes") the
light's a tattoo—shadow, sub-
stance—the city, a geometry
without an eye to thought

the city's pure light gone
crazy for itself some
textured isolate, like
concrete bleeding
light, a voice in the
lake, skin against
shoulder

Chicago 53

after Aaron Siskind

the mind into torn paper;
the sound stranded there—
take your guitar to the West
Side, tune it under the neon
canopy   the wires
stretched tight where the
first shots were fired

                   "there
is only the drama of objects
and you, watching"

2

       (*how the frame fits*

ex: the 1919 World Series as con-
fidence game   but any more so than
brick & glass, Ceres herself?

Shoeless Joe and Happy
Felsch were sportively dressed
in gray silk shirts, white duck
trousers and white shoes   they
came down the steps slowly,
their faces masked by impassivity

the texture of memory is never
brick or paint, light cracked and
prairied

the rock's skin,
the knothole resisting black
paint—throw a light at it and it
burns   CARTAGE below
Chryslers moving west

          "not some whitebread cartel"

3

unconscious for days, the city

          (or better, hand tracings

you begin to think of it as
"America"   *primitive things,*
clean fresh & alive—the dancers are
gone, handbooked into concrete
and rust, jazz peeled from the
façade

          all that happens
here happens in secret—the
dedication of this concrete, these
trees (the delicate tissues—this country
exists in oblivion—the paint blown
or clawed, the third baseman awaiting
the throw   *in the ground, we*
ate light

               memory gone
into the "paper of tomorrow"

          (light into motion
                    and

Jesus turns on the radio; he likes

AM, the big sound of wax
                              "history
is the swamp of many foundations"

4

or the city as a series of collapsing
right angles, blacked and whited
against sky   resisting blue
or "Red Door, Green Building" in-
viting shadow—*we track our own
desire*—oblivion is not some drama

if you believe the brick is corrupted,
what about the glass?   "representation
of a deep need for order" a line drawn
in green water Fred Hampton and
Mark Clark moving through the West
Side

              *eventually the story
will become glorified and the facts
more harmoniously fitted together—*

5

"when the surrealists discovered
this country, they pushed the rail-
roads west of the Mississippi"

another piece of the puzzle   he
hands you the phonebook, a paper
stele along the road   the Dan Ryan
is concrete, cut into the ground

                                        (it
grows secretly at night, light flashed
as language—what's left of the city,
"the x of it"

Rafetown Georgics

Antebellum Christi

I fold my memory into
smaller things—cheeked
snarl bonefire my feet
in blood grass self-coat
hung on a widow's hook
Time smells like piss

—————

What's this nonsense? Job shacked up with three
cheerleaders? Let's see what he gets for this.

He's cradled children at the Bend, dissected his jealousy at
the kitchen table, sliced up like some stringy animal.

Now, Job throws bottles at the moon, talks gossip on his back
porch. Lizards hop through his mind, complicated fantasies,
tar, gods, and licorice smells. Summer's hot green clouds,
chores undone; wheat slowrots at its own price.

Job calls his hands rattlesnakes, his feet water moccasins. His
mind, well water left in a glass for three days.

The land, a haggard trophy.

"Midwestern Landscape #13"

after Art Sinsabaugh

she says "frames"
then opening the
lens or "exposures"

harp threaded with
Milwaukee bins
walking south the

price of *eros* in
Des Moines a
fish sandwich in

Guckeen some
hazy swing with
the musicians' hands

onstage and moving
in sequence he took
his horn apart sd

I'm dissembling the
Midwestern states
with light   his harp

threaded with water
or a field's texture
after harvest a ditch

after snowfall the
violence done to
water Caesared and

sung *put the President
on a bus—he'll be there
by tomorrow*

"Midwestern Landscape #110"

NORTH AVENUE
BEACH: CHILDREN
& RAILING [Water,
Chicago] steel is
a ribbon is confetti
is a child's toe a
knee bent at five
o'clock   some
Seine of the Mid-
west and we are
all children shadows
behind fingers a
striped shirt, a dive
into the air bathers
and ashcans in
formation the
waterline a cuff
and picket waves
running through
white

"Midwestern Landscape #190"

the eye in a hurry to
take the South Shore
Line to the Dunes or the
expressway to Aurora—
the beginning of the
circle some concrete
Utah its trees cut by
light—*so much in the*
country, there wasn't
anything there—
nothing   (but Phil
Wrigley, that high,
airy angel) traffic of
church towers and
glass the eye frantic
to gather it all before—
prairie cantilevered
over rail lines, birds
smudged against sky-
scrapers baseball in
the gutter, CHATEAU
HOTEL and cranes
filling the horizon—
vessels cut into the
city, already dying

Dundas and Rafetown, 1997

for Paul and Mary Buss

Honey Deller farmed the Embarras
bottoms when the levee broke, emptying
the devil's washbasin. She jumped horse,
missed limb, cried, "By heckee,
I'm gettin' outta here!"

       And she did.*

———

Lester's Christmas list: two goats
and a new peacock

———

The church burned.
I saw the bolt strike.
I watched it burn all morning.

———

————————————————

* A hermaphroditic farmer who worked ground along the Embarras River a
few miles south of Ste. Marie, Illinois, Honey Deller drowned in a mid-
1930's flood.

They grew Red Top there, sold
chickens and U.S. Army peaches
before the bank went

busted. Paul Sterchi
walked to Indiana, crossed two
hardscrabble counties,
to find Helen.

———

Dean walks the August beans,
listens, measures the lamb's
quarter against his boot.

———

No stern slap of language, but a field
planted with stones, even the words broken, me
a lingering god.

Farmers and Merchants Bank

But that two-handed engine
at the door "Everybody get down!"
four men in overalls robbery
with a gun Mr. Long and I
crossing the bridge at Chester
engine at the door Elbert
Ikemire and Molly Clifton on the
floor James Cogwell opens the
safe   just chump change
Robert Bunnell enters but that
two-handed engine at the door
shotgun in his side "If
I were you, I'd—" he drops
his money bag down
to the water
down to the water
down to the water down
to Martin Stephan's Red Bud
grave and the Valley of Lost
Lutherans Mr. Long and I a tip?
Sheriff Speaks and that deputy
in hot pursuit west on the
Vandalia Road what was in
the ditches? if we had a radio
we could get that music from the
Aragon Ballroom but instead
that two-handed engine in the
ditches beebalm and milkweed and
rattlesnake plantains at the door
trespassed west of Altenburg Mr. Long
undrawered letters behind the
general store's counter: *Your father*
& I don't seem to understand you
anymore down the ravine (a few
shots were fired) that

two-handed engine at the door
one Louis Bangas of Chicago
hiding in some bushes *Why*
have you done this? Why this
need to get to Sacramento? Isn't
Frohna good enough for you? What
two-handed? one man recognized by
several Clay County residents as
Glenn Montgomery sent to the
state pen at Chester every goddamned
May 17th in the hole

"Midwestern Landscape #11"

Landfills for heart chaff have turned into a kind of American
behavior graveyard —Ben Marcus

the river ran   a
rack of outdated post-
cards

          (how it is to wander onto an abandoned movie set

or leading
a child
by the hand
through a
landscape
some old
slapstick
routine three
seconds prior to
the film's
end pin-
holed and
perpetual light
measured in
violent
percussive
chunks   *I*
focus on air—
composition
by ground
glass

"Midwestern Landscape #172"

between railroad tracks,
commerce—lines strung
through the air—*the eyes*
finally opened wide; some
happy but very rare accident
channeling water and gravel
the barge—HANNAH IN-
LAND WATERWAYS—
prairie Paris—but this city
throws bombs—melted
emulsion, skinned metal
and stoned light—carnival
machinery, popular and
junkyard implements—
gravestones and busted high
beams windshields sabotaged
car hoods cracked open and
light transmitted over water

"Midwestern Landscape #2"

like some
underground
cinema, film
flapping against
the bare bulb *I*
knew it wouldn't
be there forever
steel rush steps
cut into light a
bridge crossing
nowhere   in
flat paint, a high-
ball palmed
against bricked
sky   OLD
FORESTER its
cherries jiggling—
some metal grove,
Franz in stairway
repose

"Midwestern Landscape #9"

the rust bleeds or weeps slag
leaching towards four o'clock
I'd tried to document the lake-
front hardscrabble city prairie
in focus **NORTH AMERICAN**
COLD STORAGE horizontal
under detritus' shadow *the stone a*
shape takes the bridge falling in
place a puff and a factory rising
from the ground it's pick-ups and
earthmovers making landscape
questioned by a seven of hearts left
on the sidewalk the bride's iron
veil fine gray powder shadow
vendetta *rarely burned or dodged*
smoke shale permanent flatline
on concrete stung with light

The Book of Frogs

it's all fucking prolegomena to you, Donald

it was after the
love of that
girl and long
before my hands-
washing fetish *my
senses were those
of a child, my ears
flooded with frogs
croaking, and there
was still the smell
of bathing suits drying*
then the company'd
been brought in to root
out the frogs like some
"special- purpose entity"
some mark-to-market
accounting of the frog
plague beginning in
that April song they
arrived in their cunning
as scaly-backed reptiles
in the blue Missouri sun-
shine though my friend
says: sky blue is *not* the
color of the sky; blue is
the color of the poisonous
respiration of certain frogs
who've gone down into the
muck impediments to
his'try navigation used
to be an act of the body—
it's a sad truth, he said &
it all made us nostalgic

for winter and we kept
won'drin how much this
was gonna cost it made
us nostalgic for the slimy
bacteria and we all kept won'
drin how much this was
gonna cost it made us
nostalgic for Tupelo and
we all kept won'drin how
much this was gonna cost
and what's that up your
sleeve now, Ken Lay, your

E is spinning your head
too like a vote counter's
cartoon skull in Salt Lake
                    (cue the chorus

> *O Frogman, you know*
> *certain river birds eat*
> *golden frogs with gusto*

shake hands with a Republican
and see if your hand comes
back to you or follows the
river down to Saigon, down
to Ciudad Juarez, down to
Sadr City   meanwhile back
at the ranch, Spiro Agnew
in his tight pink golf pants
(*his head's been placed in a*
contaminated drum) while
Colson places obscene
phone calls from a 'bama
diner (*the story's a dead*
horse) while John Mitchell
spills whiskey on Martha's
best tablecloth (*he muses a*
confession) and John Dean

weeps into your son's
shroud

"they coiled themselves among us"

it was very arterial (if I
may use the word) on the
bridge, a man had taken to
selling photographs of the
frogs you read the poem
and they imposed a curfew

Levitations,
the Pleasures and Terrors of

74

Topics in Experimental Photography

We are so many loose women. And drunk
on oranges. The priest canting them,

Oranges
begat oranges. On the night when he was betrayed,
he took oranges and said,
"You there! Eating
the skins of oranges!" The doors! The doors!

Timid
altar, sending incense up to Caesar. Greasy air
slick with candlelight. One of my seven arts,

peeling,

some aphasiac reassembly of light and fruit.

———

in Orbis Tertius
glass crows pry
orange skins, leave
pliant citrus bones on
windowsills in
Orbis Tertius

———

"How the ocean puts light in my eye! My daughter is
addicted to it. We go to the shore, our eyes drunk on light,
watch gulls drop and hover at a few arms' lengths.
        'Daddy,' she says, 'the sun hands the bird from my
eye to yours.'

This is what gives beauty to her eye, although she won't memorize the colors that I've given to her, primary blues and whites. Instead, she skins the sand with her plastic shovel. . . "

———

hair glazed to his red chest, shirtless
Harry Truman eats oranges on Miami Beach with
Chris Glomski and Winston Churchill, laughing,
binding their pathological scrapbooks

———

(sentences uttered with my back to
a bowl of dusty, fake fruit)   O Aphasia,

how would I love thee? open-mouthed
without sound   world grows unfamiliar
surrounds you light hands you to me   she
will only photograph my reflection   what
remains of light

its flat taste

"Snapshot of Wallace Stevens in his Garden"

heaped up   the sleeping sickness
catches me   cherry wood deaf to my surrender
stockpages and their necrotic inks   blue
dislocated from green   my eyes
drop into the mud   this suit
burns me

my maskool,
it's cool   (is this a poem?)

I could wear the moonflowers
I could go naked
but I think I'll go into the house

———

Speak, moon!

*I am the moon.
My ear is the
earth. My eye
is the buildi-
ng, scratched
by the dead o-
ak, as surely
as by the dawn.
I hear your se-
cret impleme-
nts, know the
tracks of moon-
flowers, and t-
he precious id
id id. The mud
is everything.*

———

INTRODUCTION TO THE SKULL:

The external acoustic meatus extends from the concha to the tympanic membrane.

The tympanic membrane is circular, oriented laterally, anteriorly, and inferiorly.

The auricular branch of the vagus provides sensory innervation.

the bony tympanic floor

the bony tympanic floor

the bony tympanic floor   (this is an amplification device

moving the 3 bony ossicles   (HEARING *IS* IN THE BONES!

moving the 3 bony ossicles

                                                  (the inner ear is a bony labyrinth

I'll play my drum for you now.

———

". . .I was dreaming of chokecherries, so the prison doc put me to work in his garden. I trimmed the pink ginkos. I loved those trees. I'd think to myself, how the trees hold the moonlight!

After midnight, he'd put on that guitar album, the one with the scratch, then sing along with it. Staring out from his

dark Malthusian eyes, he'd sing, 'I am the moon. My ear is
the earth. My eye is the building, scratched by the dead-
dead-dead-dead. . . '
     And there it'd stick, that goddamned record, scratched
by his voice, sure as anything. . . "

———

the moon returns my voice to me   (though
     it's not really mine

get out my garden, moon!
this is not the grass of my youth!   let me scratch
the long gray soil in the long gray spring (glass in the ground
I still bleed as always

let me defend myself   (why this garden?)
moonflowered balladeers & saints
scratching their toxic colors into the mud   words
scratching the dead tympanum

Levitations

after Aaron Siskind

to read these put your
head in a tuck—your
shoulders in a box
the masks tangible
as air muscles plied
into frame then
grayed *the*

                    sky gives way
staring into your own
shoulder (not as solid as
it seemed
                    tell your knees
you love the sky   the
sadness realizing Hi is
dead   the letters have
stopped coming   but you
now a story of falling
bodies splashing into
the air below your hip
gives way to it
explodes
                    and

what's on the water?
paper greased and alumi-
nummed down and
greened   your fingers
splitting it—a hands
down myth here

counting ribs
through
surface

            flying

into a silvered
gelatin skin your
consciousness is a
helicopter whirl
thrown against
a brickpile

you rise to
the applause of
towheaded kids on
the pier and tell
yourself *that's*
America

"Hymn to Aphrodite"

for pipe organ, two hands, guitar, reeds, and gargler

I taped the Valentine
there for you

       for you
       for love
       for my first wife (that

           collector of love's

       loose change)   for Cleveland

           (city of love)

I had a $20 bill in Cleveland once and gave it to a girl. She said, "You didn't have to do that." But I did. I said, "Lettuce for everyone!" They cheered and we had a lettuce feast right there on Chagrin Boulevard—Boston, Romaine, and Bibb. Red-sails, iceberg, and radicchio. Love's darts floated down the Cuyahoga.

———

           (my first erection
involved 3 German girls and
a chocolate
       bar)

———

she said,

the action in a man's face now
judged from the side
buglers folded down paint
in his eyes

risoris drawn into a half-smile
measured orbits descend (the hero
wounded by his own eye?)
willing or not

––––––

you didn't you
didn't you
didn't you didn't
you didn't love me

as Burt Bachrach

        once
           did

––––––

" . . .(s)he was the Earth-Mother, so figured that we
owned at least a part of her. In the half-lit passage, Karl
hefted one of her stone legs out the door. Then, the
goddamned alarm started squealing. I stuffed some trinkets
into my jacket pocket.
     'Leave 'em,' Karl said. 'The frog gods'll fuck you up
but good.'
     The passage gulped the cops' footfalls, then spit them
back at us.
     'Hold on,' Karl whispered. . . "

Three poems for Rita Figueroa

"two by knockout"

1
your hands are two bags
of Quikrete, loose
money and clenched
rags   sing
it!   we
live in a
slow time, you
said   ring the
bell and

2
toe to toes curled
and cinched against
knuckle   negative
Aphrodite   three
steps down a
rope   "oh, to
be with my baby
down in Nelson
Algren's fuck
shack," you
sang   bones
in the corner

3
a loose jaw gathers
no what? five
bucks against
that   I
would like to
be called Caesar,
get off the bus
at Western   light
my pipe with
fifty-dollar
bills   watch
Grant's head
explode in
blue flame

Country & Western

Sing me a home,

       Karl May,

              sing me a home!

Where drunken

       cowtipped whores

              play high noon pianos

for cattlemen
       strung by their garters!

              Where blue hostel

schoolmarms fuck

       horse thieves

              named Dusty and Deaf!

Where steers sing

       in German accents,

              hard short *moo*'s!

Llano

       Dallas

              El Paso

Aachen

        Gelsenkirchen

            Peenemunde

The cowboy's

        is a lone-

            some life.

not leafy or jazzsprung

for Bill Allegrezza

the eye of motion towards
change not leafy or jazz-
sprung but shade on chrome
joy greened down and keyed
in tight pedals a highway
then, something with an
odd number or a blues a
place opening imparting
its lingo never mind the bar-
barians on the roof—they're
just buying and selling sap-
lings tongues humming
some senile Latin   the man
on TV saying, I'm not truck to
that *or stock taken* the ash tree
that halted me each fall how
we look for ourselves in the
movement *I've returned to*
that point in circle jackham-
mer singing basses tuning piano
crackling he brought a pocket-
ful of sand onstage and threw it
down out of hand man in the
book said,

the fire,
against which,
the wood was cut

     o, my
invented careenings, it's where you
look for things!   I'm the paint
peeling in the southwest hall,

oranging through the ears of
trains, of men behind wheels, of
sticks in the ground

"Seven-Headed Luther"

In towers. . .

I am turned back on my own thought—I think
that I believe, but do I believe that I think? Careless
spirits hanging around the Great Reformer's statue,
spilling wine along Tyndale Drive, thought now so dear.

> Dear Katie, *the intention was not to parade*
> *his own ego, but rather insist that Christ alone*
> *was his master and everyone else a fellow pupil,*
> *apocalyptic readings a technical matter of course.*

Of course, if I sent them your head in a box, they'd listen.
Sitting in Kurt Marquardt's 3 P.M. eschatology seminar,
my plan: cut doubt from despair; remove the head with an
acetylene torch, then escape to Terre Haute, that ecumenical
> city.

> *City of God, seen from afar,* Brother Wayne
> in the shower. Damp vespers. In my room, I
> gather marginalia from Melancthon's notebook,
> pack the severed head within it, sign, *Here I stand.*

Standing under the pear tree of the Black Cloister garden,
not yet thirty. *John, I'm worn out. But faith is conceived in*
terrors of conscience. At least, in the cloaca and humilitas.
Staupitz, the teacher, answers, *Here, Martin, eat this.*

> This headless Martin speaks to faculty cottages.
> Of course, he called on God; who wouldn't? *Things*
> *are teachers. Anyone who doesn't understand substance*
> *will be unable to tease meanings out of words.*

The Word dwelt among us. Princes fell. *The Pope*
is in his castle. End of the world and hope for better

times. *We are beggars. That's the truth.* Unsettling
doctrina. At Worms, we listened through open windows.

flames   flames   flames

"Will there be square-dancing in heaven?"

(*At rise, the flash towers and sonic booms of Dearborn Street. Windfanned.* A MAN *with five gallons of gasoline.* HE *is a troubled man. Thinks of* HIS WIFE *in bed with* JEREMIAH, *that old firebug. Sometimes, a threesome with* BARUCH, *his lackey. Scrolls left in the sheetfolds. If he was a painter. He assumes these things. An imaginary line.* THE ORANGE SALAMANDERS *are real. One false move and it's back to the cotton candy farm.*)

———

Down at the firehouse, no one believed that the prosthesis factory was on fire. But I knew better. Arms. Legs. Scummed metal. A two-alarm blaze. Box of smoked glass eyeballs. Synthetic ash. Fake skin melted, vapored, sent up. Clouds over Tifton.

———

the saddest bone   the spine
although she disagrees   *Best*
to have saints' bones handy.
Can you carry a fire in your
bones? Do you believe in the
Holy Ghost?

Like I believe
in plastic surgeons.

if she was a wall
if she was a door
if she was a flock of goats
if she was a garden

I was a wall,
        and my breasts were like towers.

she plants red blooms in sky
sky waiting to cohere

———

        —Where are you?
        —What?
        —Where are you? Right now. What are you
watching? Whose voices are those?
        —Just a minute.
        —Don't turn the volume down! Those *are* voices.
They're singing. *The Enemy Below?*
        —You're nuts.
        —I am? You're in that Grand Island motel room
again, aren't you? Watching war films. I'll bet you're
smoking in bed!
        —You're nuts.
        —I am, am I?

———

My God, they've set the Lexus on fire.

———

The house was on fire and we carried out as many things as we could. I kept the household gods under my skirt. We kept going back for the novels. Paul, for his Ellery Queen mysteries. We stashed them at Ed and Marjorie's place. The whole neighborhood watched us, passed a bottle of Bacardi. They nodded appreciatively. Ed sang a couple of the old standards, "Moonlight Becomes You" and "Body and Soul." He really gives great voice.

"We'll have to leave some things," I said. "We'll never save all the self-portraits."

"How can you be so calm?" Paul asked. "How can you have forgotten the baby pictures?"

About the Author

Garin Cycholl is the author of *Blue Mound to 161*, *Nightbirds*, and *Hostile Witness*. The *Rafetown Georgics* spring from an area along the Embarras River in southeastern Illinois. He currently lives in Chicago.

Acknowledgements

Poems in this collection previously appeared with *2 River View*, *Big Bridge*, *Blue Sky Review*, *Chicago Review*, *The City Visible*, *Free Verse*, *Keep Going*, *LVNG*, *moria*, *Mudlark*, *Muse Apprentice Guild*, *New American Writing*, *New Orleans Review*, *Place*, *Seven Corners*, *Sidereality*, *Skanky Possum*, *Tin Luster Mobile*, and *–vERT*.

Index of Titles

36 on 6 by Michael Anania — 44

Antebellum Christi — 57

Blues—Silences—Stops Between — 37

"Chicago 53" — 51

Country & Western — 86

"Crazy Woman with Two Cats" — 41

Dundas and Rafetown, 1997 — 62

"Eleanor" — 50

"Epic Problems and Their Solutions" — 11

Farmers and Merchants Bank — 64

flames   flames   flames — 92

"Fld.wrk" — 29

"Hymn to Aphrodite" — 82

Levitations — 80

Long Songs of North Carolina — 27

"Midwestern Landscape #11" — 66

"Midwestern Landscape #110" — 60

"Midwestern Landscape #13" — 58

"Midwestern Landscape #190" — 61

Much New Jazz — 48

"Museum for a Small City" — 25

not leafy or jazzsprung — 88

Pantoum — 12

sand fort — 23

Seven-Headed Leather — 90

"Snapshot of Wallace Stevens in His Garden — 77

"The Americans" — 13

Three for Rita Figueroa — 84

Topics in Experimental Photography — 75

"Town Hall Concert" — 46

"Travels through North and South Carolina" — 21

why not then—buy — 43

Current and Forthcoming Books

Edging, Michelle Noteboom, 2006.
The City Visible: Chicago Poetry for the New Century,
       Eds. William Allegrezza and Raymond Bianchi,
       2007.
Rafetown Georgics, Garin Cycholl, 2008.
Holograms/Ologrammi, Marcello Frixione. Trans.
       Joshua Adams and Joel Calahan, forthcoming.
The Bone Folders, T.A. Noonan, forthcoming.
map of the hydrogen world, Steve Halle, forthcoming.

Cracked Slab Books was started to provide an
outlet for experimental poetry and mixed
media works. With the aim of publishing at
least two books a year, Cracked Slab Books is
dedicated to promoting new American
writers and to introducing the English-
speaking world to interesting international
poetry and mixed media work.

Editor: William Allegrezza
Publisher: Raymond Bianchi

For more information, please visit our web site:
http://www.crackedslabbooks.com

Cracked Slab Books
PO Box 1070
Oak Park, IL 60302
USA